SOUTH
KOREA

ROB BOWDEN

Facts On File, Inc.

TITLES IN THE COUNTRIES OF THE WORLD SERIES:
ARGENTINA • AUSTRALIA • BRAZIL • CANADA • CHILE
CHINA • EGYPT • FRANCE • GERMANY • INDIA • INDONESIA
ITALY • JAPAN • KENYA • MEXICO • NIGERIA • POLAND
RUSSIA • SOUTH KOREA • SPAIN • SWEDEN • UNITED KINGDOM
UNITED STATES • VIETNAM

South Korea

Copyright © 2006 by Evans Brothers Limited

Facts On File, Inc.
132 West 31st Street
New York NY 10001

Library Cataloging-in-Publication Data

Bowden, Rob.
  South Korea / Rob Bowden.
    p. cm. — (Countries of the world)
  Includes index.
  ISBN 0-8160-6013-4
  1. Korea (South) I. Title. II. Countries of the world (Facts
On File, Inc.)
  DS902.B68 2005
  951.95–dc22   2005052887

Facts On File books are available at special discounts when purchased in bulk quantities for businesses, associations, institutions, or sales promotions. Please call our Special Sales Department in New York at (212) 967-8800 or (800) 322-8755.

You can find Facts On File on the World Wide Web at http://www.factsonfile.com.

Printed in China by Leo Paper Products Ltd.

10 9 8 7 6 5 4 3 2 1

Editor: Clare Weaver
Designer: Jane Hawkins
Photographs: Rob Bowden
Map artwork: Peter Bull
Charts and graphs: Encompass Graphics, Ltd.

First published by Evans Brothers Limited, 2A Portman Mansions, Chiltern Street, London W1U 6NR, united Kingdom.

This edition published under license from Evans Brothers Limited. All rights reserved.

Endpapers (front): The sprawling port complex of Busan, one of the largest and busiest ports in the world.
Title page: A crowded street in central Seoul.
Imprint and Contents pages: The densely populated center of Seoul extends beyond the Han River to the foothills of the surrounding mountains.
Endpapers (back): Rice fields dominate this agricultural valley in the central-western region of South Korea, near Jeongeup.

The colors of the South Korean flag represent the philosophical idea of yin and yang: Blue is yin, which is dark and cold, while red, which is yang, is bright and hot. The four black symbols, called *kwae*, represent heaven, fire, water and earth.

South Korea's capital, Seoul, is a thriving global city and the driving force behind the growth of the whole economy.

South Korea is a country of remarkable contrasts, where ancient palaces are found alongside state-of-the-art skyscrapers and local traditions coexist with ultramodern lifestyles. A fast-changing economy, spectacular landscapes, a unique culture and a fascinating history all add to the intrigue of this northeast Asian nation.

GLOBAL LEADER

At the time of its founding as a republic in 1948, South Korea was a predominantly agricultural nation and one of the poorest countries in the world. In remote parts of the country, evidence of this former lifestyle still exists, but for the majority of South Koreans life is now very different. Today, South Korea is a thriving economic force and,

PROVINCES AND MAIN CITIES

besides Japan, the only Asian nation in the Organisation of Economic Co-operation and Development (OECD), a grouping of 30 of the world's leading economies. By focusing on key economic sectors, South Korea has established itself as a global leader in the manufacture of consumer and industrial electronics, in vehicle production and as the world's leading shipbuilder. By 2002, South Korea had become the world's twelfth-biggest exporter by value, ahead of economies such as Russia, Spain, Sweden and Australia. Despite a regional economic slowdown in 1997, South Korea has continued its spectacular economic growth, expanding gross domestic product (GDP) by an annual average of 5.2 percent from 1994 to 2003, twice the OECD average.

The impact of South Korea's success is evident far beyond its borders. Many of South Korea's leading manufacturers have become household names across the world, such as the electronics companies Samsung and LG (Lucky Goldstar) and the car producers Hyundai and Kia. The results of the country's economic turnaround have been incredible. From being one of the world's poorest nations, South Korea now enjoys a standard of living equivalent to that of much of Europe or North America. In 2003, average incomes in South Korea were equivalent to around 78 percent of the European and OECD average and higher than those in Greece or Portugal.

The transformation is clear to see in the cities. Evening streets buzz with the noise of people enjoying a night out; shopping plazas heave with bargain hunters; and theatergoers line up to see movies and plays. In fact, at first glance, there is little to separate the major cities of South Korea, such as Seoul, Busan (or Pusan) and Ulsan from any other large city in the developed world.

KEY DATA

Official Name:	Republic of Korea
Area:	99,268 km^2
Population:	46,835,000 (2000 census)
Main Cities:	Seoul (capital), Busan, Daegu, Incheon, Ulsan
Official Language:	Korean
GDP Per Capita:	US$17,971*
Currency:	South Korean won (KRW)
Exchange Rate:	US$1 = 1,191 won £1 = 2,024 won

*(2003) Calculated on Purchasing Power Parity basis
Sources: *CIA World Factbook, 2004*; World Bank

Despite the incredible pace of development in South Korea, traditional culture remains strong.

KINGDOMS AND CONQUEST

For most of its past, South Korea has shared its history with North Korea, but even so, Korea was frequently divided into numerous individual states or kingdoms. These were periodically united by a dominant power before again separating. Korea's history is therefore very complex, but it is possible to identify several key periods that have had a lasting impact.

The Three Kingdoms period brought together various tribal states into three rival kingdoms – the Koguryo (founded 37 B.C.), Paekche (18 B.C.) and Silla (57 B.C.). In A.D. 668, with the support of the Chinese, the Silla kingdom united all of Korea. In the late eighth century, the Silla kingdom again divided into the three kingdoms. In 936, these were replaced by the Koryo kingdom, from which Korea gets its name. The Koryo remained in effective control until 1392, when land

---

The Silla established regional capitals and built grand palaces in the Silla capital (modern-day Kyongju) – many of which survive to this day, such as the magnificent Pulguk Temple.

reforms ushered in the new Choson dynasty – a succession of 26 monarchs who ruled until 1910. Throughout this period, Korea faced invasions from Japan and China but managed to withstand these until 1910, when Japan finally annexed the country. Japanese rule was brutal – resistance was quashed and sweeping changes were established to force Koreans into the Japanese way of life.

A COUNTRY DIVIDED

Japanese rule in Korea ended with the 1945 defeat of Japan in the Second World War. Korea came under the control of a temporary international trusteeship – the US military controlled the south, while Soviet forces controlled the north. Two opposing governments emerged and the country became divided into opposing political ideologies, neither recognizing the other. The Republic of Korea was formed in May 1948 and had the support of Western powers and the United Nations (UN) as the legitimate government in Korea. In the northern part of Korea, the People's Republic of Korea was declared in September 1948, with the support of the Soviet Union. In June 1950, northern troops launched an attack to take southern Korea by force. This marked the start of the Korean War, which lasted for three years and became one of the major conflicts of the Cold War. The south was militarily supported by the UN, while Chinese forces backed the north. An estimated 4 million Koreans lost their lives during the conflict and the country remains

A joint military parade of South Korean and US forces commemorates the retaking of Seoul during the Korean War.

divided along the 1953 cease-fire line. Today, there are renewed hopes for a unified Korea, but tensions remain strong, with both nations on military alert.

POLITICAL CHANGE

South Korea is today a stable civilian democracy, but from 1961 to 1988 the country was effectively under military rule, though elements of civilian government remained in place. General – and later, President – Park Chung Hee was the principal leader during the era of military rule. He initiated the economic transformation of South Korea, but at a cost. Personal freedoms were restricted, and the press and political opposition were suppressed. In 1972, Park rewrote the constitution and gave himself sweeping powers. This resulted in political protests that were violently put down, with hundreds of civilian casualties. Park was assassinated in October 1979 by the head of his own intelligence agency. Calls for a return to full democracy led to a revised constitution in 1980 and the election of Chun Doo Hwan in 1981. The full reinstatement of civilian government took place in 1987 when a national referendum approved yet another new constitution. The civilian government remains in place today, with a president elected by popular vote for a single five-year term.

Much of South Korea is covered in low mountainous terrain, interspersed with fertile farming valleys, such as here, near Jeongeup.

South Korea occupies the southern end of a peninsula that juts southward from China. The East Sea (Sea of Japan) separates South Korea from Japan to the east, while the Yellow Sea separates it from China to the west. Mountains, river valleys, coastal plains and hundreds of small islands form a diverse landscape, and climates range from subtropical in the south to temperate in the north.

LANDSCAPE FEATURES

NORTH KOREA

Lake Paro

Sea of Japan

Kwangju Mountains

Taebaek Mountains

Han

Charyong Mountains

Noryong Mountains

Anmyeondo Island

Yellow Sea

Geum

Sobaek Mountains

Nakdong

▲ Mt. Jiri (1,915m)

Yeongsan

Seomjin

Korea Strait

N

Jindo Island

Jeju Strait

0   100 km
0   50 miles

Mt. Hallasan (1,950m) ▲

Jeju-do

LAND OF MOUNTAINS

South Korea is not a large country, covering a total area of just 99,268km^2 – roughly equivalent to the US state of Indiana or about one third the size of Italy. Of this area, around 70 percent consists of low mountain ranges – rising to 1,915m on the mainland and to 1,950m at Mount Hallasan, the country's highest point on Jeju-do (Cheju-do) Island. The principal mountain range is the Taebaek (Great White) range, which runs in a roughly north-to-south direction, forming a spine down the eastern flank of the country and continuing into North Korea. The Sobaek (Little White) range branches from the southern end of the Taebaek range and extends in a southwesterly direction across the center of the country. Three smaller

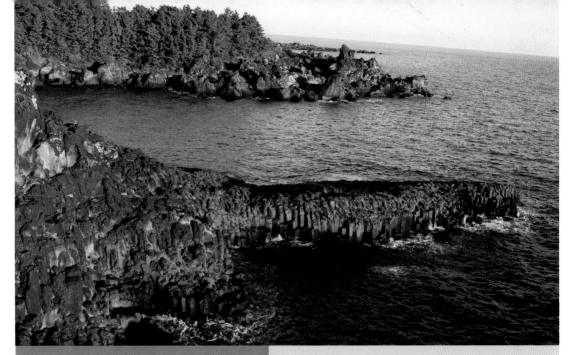

These basalt columns at Jusangjeolli on Jeju-do provide evidence of the island's volcanic origins. They were formed around 500,000 years ago by the rapid cooling of molten rock.

While most of South Korea's mountains have been formed by geological uplift, the islands of Ulleung-do and Jeju-do are actually extinct volcanoes. Jeju-do is particularly impressive and lies around 100km off the south coast. It is completely dominated by Mount Hallasan (1,950m), a shield volcano that last erupted in A.D. 1007. Evidence of its volcanic past can be found across the island, with some 400 cinder cones and around 60 lava tubes. The longest of these lava tubes has formed a cave system more than 12km long, making it one of the largest in the world. Jeju-do's volcanic soils are very fertile and the island has a thriving agricultural industry, which, besides vegetables and cereals, also produces tangerines and green tea. The volcano attracts many tourists who venture into the subterranean lava tubes, visit unusual rock formations or hike to the crater lake Baengnokdam at the summit – South Korea's only natural lake.

ranges – Noryong, Charyong and Kwangju – also branch from the Taebaek range and head westward. These have been described as the rib bones of Korea, because of the way they connect to the Taebaek spine.

RIVERS

Most of South Korea's rivers begin life amid its mountainous spine and take one of two distinctive forms, depending on which direction they drain. Those that drain eastward have a relatively short journey to the East Sea and are steep, carrying rainwater swiftly away from the mountains and drying up at other times. By contrast, those that flow westward or southward are longer and slower rivers that follow the gradual fall of the Korean Peninsula into the Yellow Sea. The most significant rivers in South Korea are all of this latter type and include the Han River (514km) which flows through the capital, Seoul; the Nakdong (525km); the Geum (401km); and the Seomjin River (212km).

ABOVE: A cruise boat carries tourists on Lake Soyang, near Chuncheon. The lake was formed in 1973 by the completion of Soyanggang Dam across the Soyang River.

RIGHT: The Yeongsan River Dam near Mokpo is 4,300m long and was built in the late 1980s. It protects upstream areas from the intrusion of tidal waters at high tide.

LIVING WITH RIVERS

The irregular flow of South Korea's rivers means they are not suited to river transportation – except in their very lowest stages, and then only by small vessels. To improve the regularity of their flow, dams have been built across most of South Korea's rivers, forming numerous artificial lakes. Besides preventing flooding – by controlling the release of water downstream – the dams also store water for irrigation and the generation of hydroelectric power (HEP). The storage lakes have also become popular recreational areas for tourists.

The west coast of South Korea experiences one of the highest tidal ranges in the world, with high and low water levels varying by as much as 8.5 meters. One effect of this is a reversal in the flow of several west coast rivers at high tide. To protect cropland and prevent flooding in estuary regions, tidal barrages have been built on some of the most affected rivers, including the Geum, Sapgyo and Yeongsan. These barrages prevent saltwater intrusion and store freshwater until it can be released at low tide. Former tidal flats that are now shielded by the barrages have been reclaimed (transformed), creating new farmland. The reservoirs formed by the barrages are also used for recreation.

COASTS AND ISLANDS

The east coast of South Korea is predominantly smooth, with only one large inlet at Pohang and several smaller inlets at Ulsan, Donghae and Sokcho. Besides these, the coastline rises sharply from the sea into the Taebaek Mountains. The southern and western coastline is, by contrast, heavily indented with numerous bays and inlets concealed between jutting peninsulas. River estuaries on the west and south coasts give way to coastal plains that continue inland as floodplains along the course of the country's major rivers. This land is heavily populated and is where most of South Korea's large settlements and farmland are found. In addition to natural plains, several artificial plains have been created through land reclamation from shallow tidal waters on the west coast. This process is continuing today with the Saemangeum Project (see page 54) – one of the world's biggest land reclamation projects.

Off the southern and western coastlines of South Korea are thousands of islands – the visible portion of hills and mountains that are slowly sinking into the sea. The majority of

ISLANDS

South Korea has around 3,000 islands, the majority of which are located off the southwest coast. The province of Jeollanam-do alone has some 2,000 islands, including 1,700 that make up the Dadohae Marine National Park – the largest in the country.

these islands are small and uninhabited, but at least 400 of the larger islands host small fishing communities and are increasingly popular with tourists. Ferry services or – for those very close to the mainland – road bridges connect inhabited islands to the mainland.

Vast tidal mudflats are exposed at low tide near Buan on the west coast. Clams and other shellfish are harvested from the mudflats.

CLIMATE AND WEATHER

South Korea's climate is heavily influenced by its proximity to the continental landmass of Asia and by the seas that surround it. In general, it can be described as a temperate climate with four distinct seasons. Long winters and summers are punctuated by much shorter spring and autumn seasons that are considered the most pleasant times of the year. Winter begins in November and is marked by cold air moving south from Siberia and Manchuria (China). By December and January, average temperatures have dropped below 0°C (32°F) over the whole country, with the exception of some coastal regions and Jeju-do. In Seoul, winter temperatures regularly drop to –8°C (18°F) and have been known to reach –24°C (–11°F).

By the end of March, winter draws to a close, and a short spring starts as warm air begins to move northward from the Pacific Ocean. Temperatures typically average 10 to 12°C (50–52°F) and rainfall is unpredictable, dependent on weather systems traveling eastward from China. The spring rains are important for the planting of rice, and when they have failed in the past, there have been serious food shortages and even famine.

By the end of May, summer ushers in a period of warm air and heavy rainfall that lasts until the end of September. South Korea typically receives around 1,250mm of precipitation a year, and around 60 percent of this falls as rain during the summer months. In general, the south and west are wettest. Southern Jeju-do receives the highest average rainfall of around 1,700mm per year. Summer temperatures in South Korea average around 25°C (77°F) but can regularly approach 30°C (86°F) in July and August.

CLIMATE

Key
11 average annual temperature (°C)

TEMPERATURE AND RAINFALL

KEY:

Temperature   Rainfall

PRECIPITATION

NORTH KOREA

Sea of Japan

1300
1200
1100
Chuncheon
1500
1400
1300
Incheon Seoul
Suwon
1200

SOUTH KOREA

Cheongju
1100
1000
Daejeon
1300
Gunsan
Jeonju
1300
1300
1400
1500
Daegu
Ulsan
Gwangju
1600
Busan
1300
Mokpo
1400

Yellow Sea

1500

N

| 0 | | 100 km |
| 0 | | 50 miles |

1600
1700
Jeju
Jeju-do

Key
1100 average annual
precipitation (mm)

The combination of high temperatur
rainfall makes the summer months very
humid, with August being an especially
uncomfortable month. An additional feature
of the summer months is the risk of typhoons
welling up from the Pacific. By the time they
reach South Korea they have normally lost
most of their strength, but periodically a
severe typhoon will strike – causing flooding,
structural damage and some loss of life. The
worst typhoon to strike the country in
modern times occurred in 1959, when 849
people were killed.

By mid-September, cool dry northern winds
from Siberia again begin to influence weather
patterns. Autumn temperatures fall to around
15°C (59°F) and the skies are clear and crisp
for several weeks, with only the occasional
shower. Koreans consider this the most
pleasant season, particularly as the hillsides
become a dazzling display of spectacular
autumn colors. Autumn is also the time of
several public holidays, the most important
of which is Chuseok, when families return to
their ancestral homes and give thanks for the
harvest from the earth.

The Taebaek Mountains become a riot of color
in autumn and attract hundreds of thousands of
tourists to marvel at nature's display.

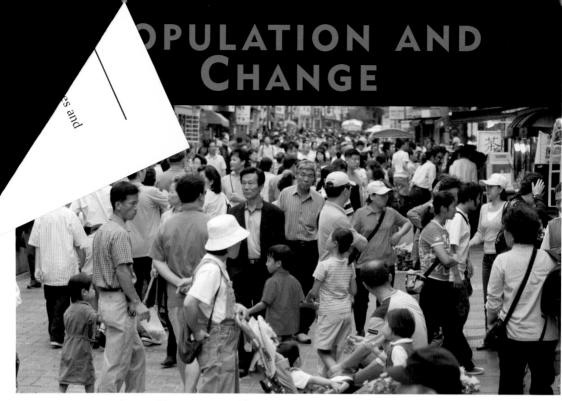

A sea of faces in central Seoul – one of the most densely populated cities in the world.

Since the end of the Korean War, the population of South Korea has increased dramatically. By 2004, it was the world's 24th most populous country. The nature of the population has also changed. More people are living in urban areas and the population is aging as people live longer and births decline.

A POPULATION BOOM

At the outset of the Korean War in 1950, South Korea had a population of around 18.9 million people – more than a million of whom are thought to have died during the war (exact figures are not known). The postwar period witnessed rapid population growth, as high birth rates coincided with lower mortality rates due to medical advances, such as the use of antibiotics. Between 1955 and 1960, the population expanded by more than 3 percent per year, due to a baby boom. By 1960, the population had reached 25 million – more than that of the entire Korean Peninsula prior to its division.

Realizing the potential pressure on living conditions and food production, the South Korean government introduced intensive family-planning policies in the early 1960s. At the same time, South Korea experienced a period of rapid economic growth and modernization. This led to later marriages and a natural inclination toward smaller families. This social change was triggered by a new

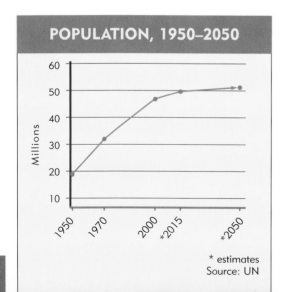

POPULATION, 1950–2050

Millions

60
50
40
30
20
10

1950 1970 2000 *2015 *2050

* estimates
Source: UN

South Koreans are starting their families later in life and limiting themselves to just one or two children on average.

481 people per square kilometer (km²). Mountainous areas in the north and east are considerably less populated, with densities typically below 50 people per km². By contrast, major urban centers have population densities that are typically higher than the national average. Busan, for example, had a population density of more than 4,800 people per km² according to the 2000 census. A particular characteristic of South Korea's population distribution is the overwhelming preeminence of the capital city, Seoul. Figures from the 2000 census show that just under 22 percent of South Koreans live in Seoul, giving it a population density of over 16,300 people per km² – among the highest in the world.

cultural value: People came to believe that the fewer children they had, the better off they would be. By 1970, population growth had slowed to 2 percent, and it fell further to around 1.5 percent during the 1980s. By 1990, South Korea's population had reached around 43 million, and although growth slowed further to less than 1 percent per year, the population had topped 48 million by 2004. South Korea's population is now entering a period of stability and is likely to grow only slowly over the coming decades, if at all. Different estimates for the year 2050 place the population at somewhere between 46.4 million and 51.3 million. Reunification with North Korea would more than likely disturb this period of stability as North Koreans moved south to benefit from the higher standards of living in South Korea.

POPULATION DENSITY

Due to its small size and large population, South Korea has one of the highest average population densities in the world at

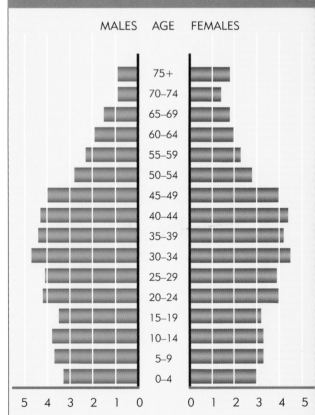

POPULATION STRUCTURE, 2004

MALES   AGE   FEMALES

75+
70–74
65–69
60–64
55–59
50–54
45–49
40–44
35–39
30–34
25–29
20–24
15–19
10–14
5–9
0–4

5 4 3 2 1 0   0 1 2 3 4 5

Percentage of total population

Source: US Census Bureau

URBANIZATION

New apartments being constructed in Suwon, one of the main satellite cities of Seoul.

South Korea is one of the most urbanized countries in Asia – with 80 percent of people living in urban areas in 2003. This compares to 65 percent in Japan and just 39 percent in China. The urbanization of South Korea has taken place very rapidly. In 1950, only 21

URBAN POPULATION

% of total population

90
80
70
60
50
40
30
20
10

1950   1970   2000   *2015

* estimate
Source: UN

percent of people lived in urban areas, but by 1975 this had more than doubled to 48 percent. The 1960s experienced especially swift urbanization. A series of five-year economic plans (beginning in 1962) created rapid industrialization and thousands of new job opportunities. At the same time, population growth was placing agricultural land under increasing pressure, so many people opted to move to the cities. During the 1970s, rural-urban migrants accounted for 55 percent of the population growth in urban areas.

Seoul and Busan bore the brunt of urbanization during the 1960s and 1970s – their populations growing by 350 and 270 percent respectively between 1960 and 1980. Their growth slowed in the 1980s and both cities have seen a decline in population since the 1990s. This decline is explained by the growth of satellite towns and cities. These developed as land in the principal cities became scarce and the cost of housing made it prohibitive for new migrants to live there. These suburbs offer cheaper housing and are well connected to the major cities by urban rail and bus services. Incheon and Suwon, for example, have become key satellite cities of Seoul and have more than doubled in population since 1985.

POPULATION REDISTRIBUTION

Although central Seoul has witnessed a gradual outmigration of people since the late 1980s, most have only moved into the immediate environs. As a result, South Korea's population remains extremely unbalanced, with just under half of all people living in the Seoul metropolitan area. This area today extends outward some 40–50km from central Seoul. Since the late 1970s, the government has been trying to encourage a redistribution of population away from the Seoul area, but generally this has had little success. Some new industrial complexes, such as the steelworks at Pohang and the chemical works at Ulsan, have succeeded in attracting significant numbers of people to the southeast of the

Most of South Korea's urban population lives in high-rise apartment complexes – such as these in Mokpo.

country. It is here that the industrial port city of Busan is situated. Around 30 percent of the South Korean population now lives in this southeast urban area. The metropolitan area around Seoul continues to grow, however, and the government will need to do much more if it is to entice people to settle in other provincial cities.

CASE STUDY
NEW SONGDO CITY

Around 64 kilometers to the south of Seoul, a new high-tech industrial city is being created on 600 hectares of land reclaimed from the Yellow Sea. By around 2015, Songdo will house major international companies, a conference center, leisure and retail facilities and homes for around 200,000 people. With close connections to Incheon International Airport (the main gateway to South Korea) and improved seaport facilities, Songdo is set to become a major center of new urban growth during the twenty-first century.

AGING SOCIETY

In 1960, only 3 percent of South Korea's population was aged over 65, and life expectancy was around 56 for women and 53 for men. Today, improvements in living conditions and in medical care mean that life expectancy is 78 for women and 71 for men. By 2003, the proportion of the population over 65 years of age had reached 8 percent. In real terms, this represents an increase in the elderly population (those over 65) from 0.75 million people in 1960 to 3.83 million by 2003. Current trends suggest that South Korea's society will age even faster in the coming decades, with 14 percent of the population over 65 years of age by 2019 and 20 percent by 2026. This means an elderly population of some 10 million people.

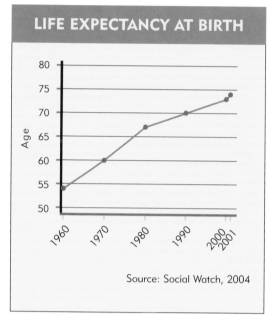

LIFE EXPECTANCY AT BIRTH

Source: Social Watch, 2004

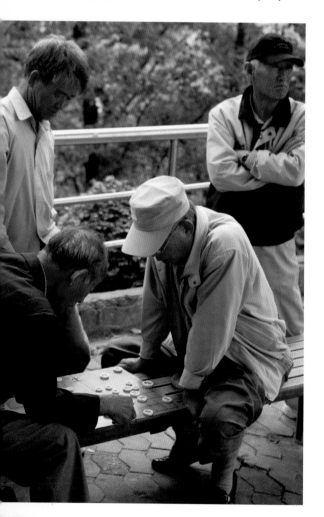

The elderly in Korean society are traditionally cared for by their children. Parents spend their earnings and savings to help their children to establish their own lives, and in return, they expect to be cared for in their later years. This pattern is changing under the pressures of modern life, higher living costs and longer life expectancies. Around 45 percent of South Koreans, for instance, now live far away from their parents' homes, making it harder for them to care for elderly parents. Parents, too, are taking the active decision to remain independent of their children and instead opting to settle in "silver towns" (retirement communities) when they retire. To fund this lifestyle, parents are now saving money while working, whereas traditionally they would have spent any income on their children. Many elderly people, however – especially those in rural areas – are unable to meet their own expenses. Their children are

These elderly men are enjoying board games in Yongdu-san Park in Busan. The elderly form a significant and growing proportion of the population.

burdened by higher costs of living (Seoul is the seventh most expensive city in the world to live in), and many find it difficult to offer support to their aging parents.

A national pensions program has been established to try to support workers when they retire, but this is not yet fully developed. As a result, people continue to work into their late 60s (longer than in some other developed economies) in order to afford to live. Health experts believe the South Korean government can no longer rely on traditional family support and needs to do more to prepare for its aging population. Another consequence of South Korea's aging population is a potential shortage of working-age people (15 to 64 years) to support the population. South Korea will either have to invite immigrants to replace the declining working population or expect people to work longer before they retire.

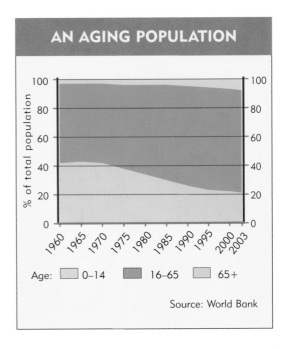

AN AGING POPULATION

% of total population

Age: ☐ 0–14 ■ 16–65 ☐ 65+

Source: World Bank

A group of preschool children enjoy a field trip in Seoul. There are concerns that not enough children are being born to provide for the future needs of an aging population.

ONE-CULTURE NATION?

South Korea's population is one of the most homogeneous in the world, with more than 99 percent of the 2003 resident population being ethnically Korean in origin. The Korean people are related to the Mongoloid racial group, which includes the Chinese and, in total, makes up around 70 percent of the world's population. Because of the Korean Penninsula's strategic position, Koreans share much in common with other regional ethnic groups – particularly those in China (especially Manchuria), Japan and Mongolia, with whom there has been historical contact through trade and conflict. For example, more than half of the words used in the Korean language are of Chinese origin.

Despite its remarkable uniformity, it would be wrong to consider South Korea a one-culture nation. It is certainly true that Korean culture is strong in its own right and continues to be well preserved, but it has also been, and still is, heavily influenced by external forces.

South Korea's population is overwhelmingly of Korean ethnic origin, making it one of the most uniform populations in the world.

Historically, these have been mainly from China, Mongolia and Japan and are seen in language, architecture and the arts. The second half of the twentieth century saw increasing Western influence – partly due to growing trade links, but more specifically as a result of US military presence in the peninsula since 1945. Ten-pin bowling and baseball, for example, have become highly popular activities, and numerous American-English words have become part of everyday language.

FOREIGNERS

The number of foreigners living in South Korea has grown rapidly in recent years – through both the influence of closer trade ties with other countries and the increasing attractiveness of South Korea as a place to live. In 1992, there were only 65,673 foreigners registered as residents in South Korea, but by the start of 2004 this number had increased to 437,014. This still represented less than 1 percent of the country's population, but it may signify an important trend toward a more multicultural society in the future.

This shoe shop is in the "Little Russia" district of Busan, where an increasing number of people from the former Soviet Union have settled.

The most significant groups of foreigners living in South Korea include the US military, the ethnic Chinese and a growing Russian population. In 2004, the US military presence in South Korea remained much as it has since the end of the Korean War, at around 37,000 personnel. This is set to decline in the coming years as control of the Demilitarized Zone (DMZ) between South and North Korea is handed back to South Korea. Ethnic Chinese officially number around 20,000, but it is estimated that tens of thousands more Chinese (perhaps as many as 80,000) work illegally in South Korea with false documents. The Chinese have settled in many places, but especially in port cities, such as Incheon and Busan, both of which have popular Chinatown districts. Seoul and Busan also have areas known as "Little Russia," because they have attracted significant Russian populations, officially numbering around 10,000. In Seoul's Little Russia, however, more realistic estimates put the number of Russians, Ukrainians and others from former Soviet states at around 50,000.

KOREANS ABROAD

The upheaval and disruption of the twentieth century prompted many ethnic Koreans to move abroad. Today, an estimated 1 million Koreans live in the United States and Canada, while another 1 million reside in Russia, 2 million in China and 800,000 in Japan. There are also smaller populations of Koreans living in South America and Europe.

These people are learning Chinese script in a traditional school. The Korean language and script are heavily influenced by Chinese.

A rice harvester busy in the paddy fields. Rice is the main grain crop of South Korea and is grown intensively on low-lying and level land.

South Korea has undergone one of the most impressive economic transformations of any country in the last 50 years, shifting from a rural economy based on farming and fishing to one that specializes in heavy industries and high-tech manufactured goods. It must now consolidate its position and work toward closer regional and global integration if the country is to sustain its economic miracle.

RURAL ORIGINS

Unlike many other economies of comparable size, South Korea does not possess a wealth of natural resources. In fact, besides coal and limestone deposits in the Taebaek Mountains and minor deposits of other minerals (including tungsten, gold, silver, molybdenum, zinc, copper and lead), South Korea is mineral poor. Land and water have, historically, formed the basis of the economy, an economy rooted in farming and fishing. As recently as 1970, agriculture (farming and fishing) employed 50 percent of the workforce and contributed 27 percent of national income. By 2001, this had fallen considerably, to around 10 percent of the workforce and just 4 percent of national income. Despite this decline, agriculture remains an important element of the economy – worth around US$37 billion in 2002.

FARMING

Rice is by far the most significant crop in South Korea. In 2004, the country was the world's twelfth-largest producer of paddy rice, with a total production of 6,351,000 tonnes.

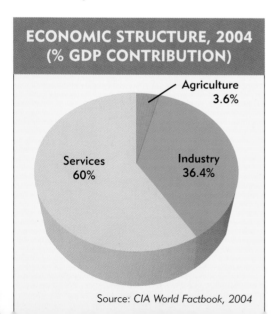

ECONOMIC STRUCTURE, 2004 (% GDP CONTRIBUTION)

Agriculture 3.6%

Services 60%

Industry 36.4%

Source: CIA World Factbook, 2004

Rice is the mainstay of the Korean diet, accounting for 30 percent of dietary intake in 2002. Other important farm produce includes pork and an incredible variety of vegetables. Wheat, barley, beans (especially soybeans), pulses (such as peas) and fruits are also cultivated. The majority of farm produce is consumed within South Korea, but small quantities of higher-value crops, such as tangerines, chestnuts and ginseng, are exported. Though self-sufficient in rice and some vegetables, South Korea must import an increasing amount of food to support its growing population. In fact, by the late 1990s, up to 75 percent of South Korea's food crop needs were imported. Farming in South Korea faces a difficult future both because of the limited land on which to expand production and the shortage of labor in rural areas. Domestic farm produce is also facing competition from cheaper produce imported from countries such as China.

Dry farming
Mixed farming
Wet farming
Mixed commercial farming
Island farming

MAIN FARMING AREAS

The root crop ginseng is valued for its use in traditional medicine. South Korea is said to grow the best ginseng in the world.

Ginseng is a root crop believed to have numerous health-giving properties, including the ability to give strength and to promote fertility and a long life. It is called *insam* in Korean, meaning "man root," because it is often shaped like a person. South Korean ginseng is considered the best in the world. White ginseng (*baeksam*) is the most common and is harvested after about four years' growth. Red ginseng (*hongsam*) is more valued and is harvested after six to seven years. Because of its health benefits and the fact it takes so long to grow, ginseng is a prized commodity in South Korea. The government even limits how much is allowed out of the country. When wild *insam* is occasionally found it sells for thousands of dollars.

FISHING

Fishing contributes less than 1 percent of national income directly to the economy, but its importance far outweighs this figure. Indirectly, the fishing industry encourages many other industries: Boatbuilding and repairs, marine electronics and engineering, net and gear manufacture, and transportation and marketing services are examples. The fisheries also provide a vital source of food to the population, helping to ensure food security and reducing the need for imports.

In 2002, Korea ranked as the thirteenth-largest marine fishery in the world, producing 1,663,289 tonnes – around 2 percent of the world total. Inland fisheries are minor by comparison, but aquaculture (the farming of fish rather than catching them in the wild) is significant. In 2002, South Korea's aquaculture production ranked sixth in the world. More than 50 fish species, 15 types of shellfish, and various seaweeds are now farmed in marine fish farms. The entire fishing industry employs some 250,000 people, with about a quarter of

these jobs in the growing aquaculture sector. Since 1982, the government has been reforming the fishing industry to create a more sustainable industry for the future. Landing quotas (limits) were introduced in 1987 to preserve stocks, and since 1994, the government has been buying up older, environmentally harmful boats in an effort to reduce and modernize the fishing fleet. In 2002, South Korea's fishing fleet numbered just under 95,000 vessels.

EARLY INDUSTRIALIZATION

Prior to the twentieth century, industry in Korea was limited to small-scale cottage industries and crafts producing goods for a wealthy elite. During the Japanese occupation (1910–45), industries were developed to take advantage of the peninsula's mineral resources, but over 90 percent were located in what is now North Korea. At the time of South Korea's founding in 1948 there was little industrial infrastructure, and most of this was destroyed during the Korean War (1950–53). In the immediate postwar period, small manufacturing industries were established in South Korea in order to provide clothing,

Fishing is a large-scale commercial industry in South Korea, but fleets and workers are being reduced due to pressure on ocean stocks.

shoes, household goods and supplies that would otherwise have to be imported. Larger industries – including cement manufacture, energy production, plastics, and oil refining – followed to meet South Korea's emerging energy and construction needs. However, it was the first of the five-year economic plans launched in 1962 that really set off South Korea's industrialization.

EXPORT-ORIENTED INDUSTRIALIZATION

With virtually no natural resources and a small and impoverished domestic market, the South Korean government embarked on a policy of export-oriented industrialization as a way to promote economic growth. This meant utilizing South Korea's plentiful supply of cheap labor and good ocean links to produce goods for the export markets. Initially, this strategy worked well, and industrial production grew by an annual average of 17 percent in the 1960s. Exports, mainly of manufactured goods, increased even faster – at around 36 percent per year between 1961 and 1972. By the early 1970s, however, labor costs were rising and manufacturing was becoming increasingly mechanized. Relying on exports from exports from labor-intensive industries to boost economic growth became questionable. As a result, the government switched its focus to capital-intensive heavy and chemical industries.

The labor-intensive textile industry was one of the first to help South Korea's economy boom in the 1960s and 1970s. Today, it is less important, but still very productive.

KEY INDUSTRIES

HEAVY AND CHEMICAL INDUSTRIES

South Korea built its heavy and chemical industries by importing raw materials, using its own skilled labor force and rapidly developing technical and engineering expertise. By the end of the 1970s, the heavy and chemical industries accounted for around half of all South Korea's exports. The key industries in this sector were petrochemicals, steel, automobiles and home appliances, as well as shipbuilding.

The Hyundai shipyard in Ulsan is the largest in the world, capable of producing more than 70 ships at any one time.

CASE STUDY
SHIPBUILDING

One of South Korea's greatest economic success stories is its shipbuilding industry. From virtually nothing in the early 1970s, South Korea overtook Japan in 2004 to become the world's leading shipbuilder. Of all the orders for world shipping taken in 2004, South Korea accounted for 40 percent, compared with Japan at 25 percent and China at 14 percent. In particular, South Korea has managed to capture the market for specialized shipping, such as tankers for transporting liquefied natural gas (LNG). The three main shipbuilding companies in South Korea captured almost 90 percent of orders for LNG tankers in 2004. Across the Yellow Sea, China's shipbuilding industry is growing fast and poses a threat to South Korea's dominance. To overcome this, South Korean companies are developing new ship designs. One such project involves a supervessel that could carry 10,000 individual cargo containers. If built, this would be sufficient to transport around 30 million pairs of sports shoes!

South Korea has become a specialist at producing high-tech tankers, such as the one at right, for transporting liquefied natural gas (LNG) around the world.

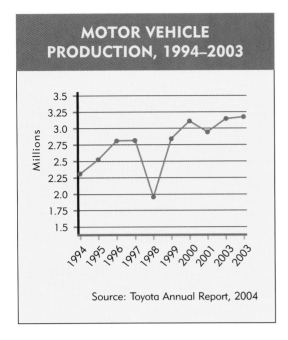

MOTOR VEHICLE PRODUCTION, 1994–2003

Source: Toyota Annual Report, 2004

Heavy and chemical industries remain a significant element of South Korea's economy today and many of the companies involved, such as Hyundai, Daewoo, Kia and Samsung, have become household names around the world. Having established themselves in South Korea, several of these companies are now looking overseas in order to further expand their business. For example, in 2004, the car producer Kia agreed a deal to invest in a new production plant in Slovakia, capable of producing 390,000 cars a year.

STRUCTURAL REFORMS

By the early 1980s, South Korea had emerged as one of the leading newly industrialized countries (NICs) in Asia. The NICs of Asia (including Singapore, Hong Kong and Taiwan) became known as the "Asian Tigers" due to their phenomenal economic growth, but by the 1980s their position was being challenged by new emerging economies. In order to maintain economic growth, South Korea implemented a series of structural reforms to its economy. These reforms were designed to make international trade easier, but they also opened up local markets to foreign products, thus challenging the position of local suppliers. In response, the South Korean economy improved its efficiency so that its goods remained competitive in international markets. The government also recognized the need to encourage investment in industrial technology as computers became more important and automation increased. These changes transformed the economy yet again, and by the mid-1980s South Korea was emerging as one of the world's leading high-tech economies.

MAJOR TRADING PARTNERS (% OF VALUE), 2003

EXPORTS

China 18.2%
Others 47.4%
USA 17.8%
Hong Kong 7.6%
Japan 9%

IMPORTS

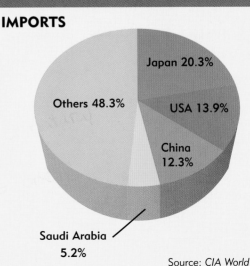

Japan 20.3%
Others 48.3%
USA 13.9%
China 12.3%
Saudi Arabia 5.2%

Source: CIA World Factbook, 2004

HIGH-TECH ECONOMY

South Korea's high-tech industry is focused on telecommunications, consumer electronics, computers, and electrical components, such as semiconductors. As with its heavy industries, several of South Korea's high-tech companies have become leading global brands – for example, Samsung and LG (Lucky Goldstar). Samsung has been particularly successful in the mobile phone industry, and in 2004, it sold 86.5 million phones (a 55 percent increase on sales in 2003), accounting for 13.7 percent of the global market. In total, Samsung made profits of over US$10 billion in 2004.

The success of South Korea's high-tech industry is attracting overseas companies to locate in or purchase source components from South Korea in order to take advantage of its highly skilled workforce and expertise in this sector. The US companies Hewlett-Packard and Motorola, for example, both purchase memory chips from Samsung. Other companies, including IBM, Microsoft, Sony and Phillips, have close ties with South Korea's high-tech companies. A group of 13 German universities

CASE STUDY
LG ELECTRONICS

LG Electronics is among the world's leading electronics companies, employing some 64,000 people in 76 countries. It has established global market leadership in numerous electronic products, including air conditioning units, optical storage devices (CD and DVD writers), DVD players, microwave ovens and vacuum cleaners. It is also among the top five producers of monitors, digital displays and mobile phones. LG has set itself the target of becoming one of the top three global electronics companies by 2010, and with sales more than doubling between 1998 and 2003 (mostly due to export sales), it is well placed to achieve this. In the fast-changing world of technology, however, research and development of new products is essential to stay ahead of the competition. To this end, LG is leading the development of technologies that expand the capabilities of mobile phones and is also exploring the idea of "home networking." This allows home appliances, such as the television, dishwasher, air conditioner, microwave oven, and even the vacuum cleaner, to be controlled from a single console. It would even be possible to communicate with the appliances remotely by using your mobile phone. You could come home to a perfectly warmed house, with your favorite music playing and your dinner already cooked!

These appliances are part of a new "home network" technology being developed by LG Electronics.

GNI PER CAPITA (US$)

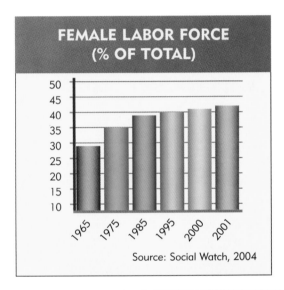

Source: World Bank

is even establishing a joint Korean-German Institute of Technology (KGIT) in Seoul. When completed in 2008, KGIT will allow these two high-tech economies to share research and development in areas such as information technology, nanotechnology and biotechnology.

SERVICE INDUSTRIES

As South Korea's economy has matured, an increasing proportion of the labor force has been employed in the service sector. This sector includes industries such as banking, retail, tourism and transportation, as well as general office work. In 2001, the service sector accounted for 62 percent of employment in South Korea and 61 percent of national income. The sector can expect further growth in the coming years, as higher disposable incomes and greater leisure time among South Koreans leads to an increased demand for their services.

"Lotte World" in Seoul combines retail and leisure facilities in a single complex. A growing number of service industry complexes such as this are being developed in South Korea.

FEMALE LABOR FORCE (% OF TOTAL)

Source: Social Watch, 2004

INTERNATIONAL TOURIST ARRIVALS

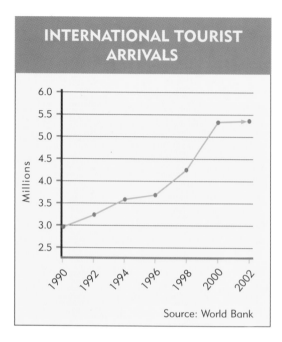

Source: World Bank

TOURISM

One of the newest growth sectors in the South Korean economy is tourism. Cheaper international travel and growing prosperity among South Korea's neighbors (especially China and Japan) have helped to almost double the number of international tourists visiting South Korea between 1990 and 2002. Domestic tourism by South Koreans has also increased dramatically, to the extent that 70–80 percent of the population make more than one visit a year to one of the country's major tourist areas.

The majority of tourism in South Korea focuses on the country's cultural and natural assets, both of which the government is active in preserving. The Korean Folk Village near Suwon, for example, has been established as a living museum to celebrate and preserve historical lifestyles and traditions. Tourists can explore traditional Korean homes, watch traditional craftspeople at work and enjoy displays of traditional dancing and acrobatics. Elsewhere, national and provincial parks have been established to protect regions of natural beauty while opening them to controlled tourism. Bukhansan National Park on the

CASE STUDY
INSADONG

The growth in tourism (domestic and international) in South Korea has prompted many cities to develop specific tourist districts. One of these is Insadong in the capital, Seoul. A mainly pedestrianized area of the city, Insadong retains many old buildings that have today been turned into traditional restaurants and teahouses. Curio shops, art galleries, antique stores, street vendors and public entertainment are also found here. The area is popular with foreign and local tourists, and it is also a trendy retreat for Seoulites to escape the buzz of the city.

Tourists hunt for Korean souvenirs in the popular tourist district of Insadong in Seoul.

SPORTS TOURISTS

Hosting major sporting events has boosted South Korea's tourist industry. Seoul staged the Olympics in 1988, and in 2002, South Korea and Japan jointly hosted the World Cup soccer finals, an event that attracted an estimated 150,000 tourists.

A mural painted on a construction fence commemorates the 2002 World Cup finals, when soccer riveted South Korea's attention. The event attracted thousands of new tourists.

outskirts of Seoul and Seoraksan National Park near Sokcho are among the most visited national parks, respectively attracting around 4 million and 5 million visitors each year.

Another popular tourist destination is the island of Jeju-do off the south coast of the peninsula. Known as the Hawaii of Korea because of its beaches and palm trees, the island offers a complete escape from the more frantic pace of life on the mainland and is only an hour's flight from Seoul. Besides its beaches and the impressive volcanic scenery of Mount Hallasan, the island has traditional working villages and a popular conference center that hosts national and international events.

A *harubang* (village guardian) at the Seongup folklore preservation zone on Jeju-do – one of the island's top tourist attractions.

JEJU-DO

Jeju-do is such a popular getaway that there are 55 flights a day between Seoul and Jeju City (the capital of the island). A further 46 daily flights link Jeju City to other cities on the mainland.

The South Korean currency, the won, had to be devalued during the Asian economic crisis of 1997 and has not yet recovered its former strength.

ECONOMIC OVERVIEW

Having had four decades of strong and virtually uninterrupted growth, South Korea's economy suffered a major setback in 1997 that threw it into a period of crisis. Foreign investors had, up until this point, poured millions of dollars into the economy of South Korea and other emerging Asian economies in the hope of "cashing in" on their incredible economic performance. The financial sector in many of these countries was not fully regulated, however. This resulted in large sums being invested in high-risk and poor-quality investments. In 1997, investors in

Thailand began to withdraw their money as they realized the economy there was underperforming. This created an atmosphere of uncertainty and panic across Southeast Asia that quickly spread to South Korea. Investors withdrew millions of dollars; companies were facing financial ruin; and thousands of jobs were lost as businesses closed or restructured. The impact on the economy was dramatic. The South Korean won plummeted in value from a 1996 exchange rate of around 800 won to the dollar to 1,400 won by 1998. Unemployment more than tripled from 2 percent in 1996 to 7 percent in 1998 (as high as 15.9 percent among 15–24 year olds). The net result of the crisis was that South Korea's economy actually contracted in 1998 by almost 7 percent.

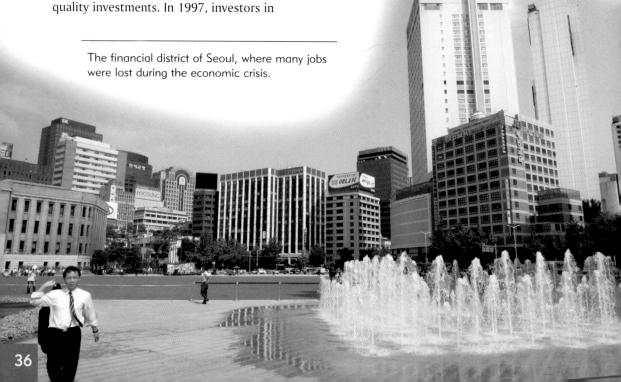

The financial district of Seoul, where many jobs were lost during the economic crisis.

RECOVERY AND REFORM

The International Monetary Fund (IMF) stepped in to prevent South Korea's financial crisis form spiraling out of control. It set up a series of reforms aimed at restoring confidence in the markets of Southeast Asia. South Korea was quick to implement the necessary reforms, and in 1999, the economy registered economic growth of 9.5 percent. Growth has continued ever since, albeit at a

Consumer confidence and increased spending show that South Korea's economy is back to full growth following the 1997 economic crisis.

slower rate than before the crisis, and by 2003 unemployment had fallen to around 3 percent. The economy is well on the way to full recovery, but reforms to the banking and business sectors continue, in an effort to avoid a repeat of the 1997 crisis.

CASE STUDY
YELLOW SEA ECONOMIC BASIN

One of South Korea's recovery strategies following the crisis of 1997 has been to improve regional economic cooperation. This would strengthen and diversify the economy, making it less vulnerable to future shocks and less reliant on single large markets (such as the United States, a major market for South Korea). The Yellow Sea Economic Basin (YSEB) is one such regional project in which South Korea is playing a central role. China, Japan and North Korea will join South Korea in making up the nations of the YSEB, a region extending 200km inland from the rim of the Yellow Sea. In total, the YSEB has a population of more than 200 million

people, including 60 cities of more than 1 million. In 2001, the YSEB had a potential market valued at US$1.3 trillion. South Korea is developing New Songdo City on an area of reclaimed coastline as the centerpiece of the YSEB (see page 21). With major port facilities and Incheon International Airport on its doorstep, it is hoped New Songdo City will become a key hub for the YSEB. If successful, the YSEB will rival other economic powers, such as the United States and the European Union. But such success is dependent not only on creating the necessary infrastructure, but on overcoming political differences between the member countries.

ENERGY AND TRANSPORTATION

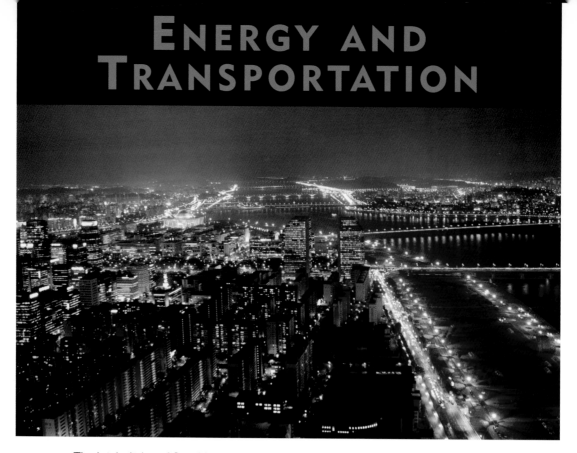

The bright lights of Seoul by night are a clear indication of South Korea's energy consumption.

South Korea's rapidly growing economy places enormous strains on the country's infrastructure as higher living standards demand more energy and better transportation. In a country that is 70 percent mountainous and that has few natural energy sources, this presents a considerable challenge to the government.

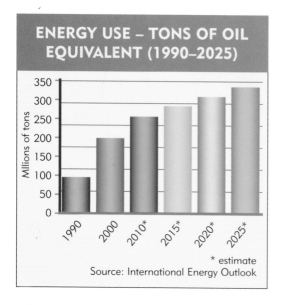

ENERGY USE – TONS OF OIL EQUIVALENT (1990–2025)

Millions of tons

1990, 2000, 2010*, 2015*, 2020*, 2025*

* estimate
Source: International Energy Outlook

ENERGY HUNGRY, ENERGY POOR

South Korea is an energy-hungry country, driven by the unparalleled growth in its economy and the rise in personal incomes. Between 1970 and 2001, for example, average energy consumption per person increased by 788 percent. This compares with increases of 66 percent in Japan, 7 percent in the United Kingdom, and 5 percent in the United States and a decline of 10 percent in Denmark over the same period. For an energy-hungry country, South Korea is lacking in significant energy sources. There are deposits of coal in the Taebaek Mountains, but these are of low quality and only suited for domestic heating. Hydroelectric power (HEP) is harnessed from the country's major rivers, but in 2002, this contributed only 1.1 percent of total electricity generation. The bulk of South Korea's energy must, therefore, come from imported sources.

ENERGY DEPENDENCE

In 2003, South Korea was the world's fifth-largest net importer of petroleum and the world's second-largest importer of liquefied natural gas (LNG). These two energy sources account for approximately 55 and 10 percent of total energy consumption in South Korea. Coal accounts for a further 21 percent – again, nearly all of it imported. This makes South Korea highly dependent on world energy markets to meet its energy needs and vulnerable to changes in world prices. In order to overcome the problems of energy dependence, South Korea is investing in numerous energy projects. Within South Korea, for example, there has been heavy investment in nuclear energy since 1977 to replace coal and oil-fired power stations. By 2004, there were 18 operational nuclear power stations and several more in various stages of construction.

NUCLEAR POWER

Electricity generated by nuclear power in South Korea is expected to increase by 70 percent between 2000 and 2020.

South Korea is also investing in energy resources overseas in an effort to secure energy supplies for the continued growth of its economy. The Korean National Oil Corporation (KNOC) has oil production fields in Argentina, Peru, Yemen, Venezuela, Libya, Vietnam and the North Sea. The government says that by 2010, KNOC should supply 10 percent of the country's oil needs. The state power company KEPCO (Korea Electric Power Corporation) also has investments in several Australian coal mines, providing a substantial proportion of South Korea's total coal demand.

All of South Korea's gasoline must be imported, making it very vulnerable to fluctuations in global oil prices.

RENEWABLE ENERGY

Besides limited hydroelectric power, South Korea has no significant sources of renewable energy. Solar power is receiving considerable attention as the technology becomes cheaper and more efficient. In Daegu, for example, Kyungpook National University is pioneering a "solar campus" to demonstrate the capabilities of different solar technologies in meeting future energy needs. Solar power is also being used in small-scale operations and remote locations where it can be the most cost-efficient form of generating electricity or heat. Wind power is also expanding, though from a very low level. In 2002, there were just 11 wind farms (or individual turbines) – with the majority being on Jeju-do. Being a peninsula, however, South Korea has considerable wind potential from oceanic winds – particularly in the southwest and the southern islands. By 2004, new wind power schemes were under development with German and Japanese companies that have expertise in this area.

ROAD TRANSPORTATION

As in many in other developed economies, higher incomes have led to a boom in car ownership in South Korea. By 2001, there were some 8.9 million cars and a further 3.7 million trucks and buses on the country's roads. The majority of these vehicles have been added since the 1980s. The number of cars per 1,000 people has increased from just 6.5 in 1980 to 48.4 in 1990 and 171 by

GRIDLOCKED

South Korea's traffic density is around 120 vehicles per kilometer of road – double that of Japan and the United Kingdom, and four times that of Denmark and the United States.

2000. This incredible growth means South Korean roads are today extremely busy, and congestion, accidents and traffic-related pollution have become major issues.

South Korea's road network has expanded rapidly since the 1950s and today covers around 87,000km. The most important roads in the country are the 2,000km of expressways that radiate out from Seoul to other major cities. These also link other key cities, such as Ulsan and Busan in the south. The expressways were begun in 1967 and mostly completed by 1976. They had a dramatic impact on the country, bringing every point of the nation to within 24 hours' traveling time. This allowed greater movement

This new facility – being built at Nanjido on the outskirts of Seoul – will create energy from the city's waste.

of industrial and agricultural products. It also promoted higher levels of urbanization, as people could move to the cities with considerably greater ease. Road construction continues rapidly in South Korea, with new urban expressways in major cities and new

A network of expressways head out of Seoul, connecting it to other cities in the country. This one follows the route of the Han River.

highways linking to more remote regions of the country, such as the mountainous east.

CASE STUDY
HOP ON THE BUS

Buses are the main mode of intercity public transportation in South Korea, and an extensive and frequent system covers all major routes. Express services have limited stops and are designed to offer fast transit between key towns and cities. They radiate out from Seoul along the country's expressways and are mainly used as a cheaper alternative to the train. Intercity bus services use regular roads and are either express services with limited stops or regular services stopping at any point in all towns on route. These intercity bus services are especially important to people living in rural areas and to the elderly, because people in these groups are often in the lower income bracket and less likely to have their own private motor vehicles.

Bus services are one of the most popular forms of transportation in South Korea, providing vital links to those places not on the rail network.

RAIL NETWORK

The rail network in South Korea is constrained by geography, so it is located mainly in the less mountainous western and southern portions of the country. This is also where the majority of the population lives. By 2004, the total network covered 3,388km, including new lines built to carry high-speed KTX trains that began running between Seoul and Mokpo and Busan in March of that year. It is hoped that the KTX services, which can travel at 300km per hour, will help to revive South Korea's money-losing railroad system. Passenger numbers are not a problem, with demand rising by around 60 percent over the period 1994–2004, but the rail system has been unable to cope with this. The new KTX trains and routes are predicted to allow a 340 percent increase in passenger capacity from 180,000 per day to 620,000.

URBAN RAIL

In 1971, Seoul began construction of a subway (metro) system to provide fast and efficient travel across the city, and to relieve congestion from the city's roads. The system has now grown to cover close to 500km of track split over eight lines, with further lines (and extensions to existing ones) planned by 2010. The system is fully automated and is used by millions of people every day. Busan, Daegu, Incheon and Daejeon have all

TRANSPORT NETWORKS

—— Main road

······ Railroad

✈ International airport

followed the example of Seoul and introduced subway lines to cope with their own urban transportation needs. High-tech trains are also being developed for 2010. These will travel up to 30 percent faster, allowing more frequest service of the rail network and therefore higher passenger numbers.

Metro (or subway) systems provide the easiest form of transportation in South Korea's larger cities, and the networks are expanding rapidly.

INTERNATIONAL LINKS

With the land link to Asia blocked by North Korea, South Korea's international transport links are by sea and air, and both are very well established. While sea links are predominantly for freight cargo, they not only provide for international shipping but also link the mainland to South Korea's numerous islands. The principal ports include Busan (the fifth-busiest port in the world), Pohang, Incheon and Gwangyang – with others, such as Donghae, Mokpo and Jeju also being important. Facilities at the principal ports are among the best in the world for container and bulk cargo handling, and their usage continues to grow dramatically. Between 2000 and 2002, for example, the volume of

The main container port in Busan is the busiest in the country and one of the busiest in the world.

container freight handled increased by 28 percent. Growth in the United States and Japan, by comparison, was just 5 and 3 percent respectively. Passenger ferries operate from many of South Korea's ports, serving island communities and providing an important tourist route to Jeju-do. Larger ports also provide international ferries to China, Japan and Russia.

South Korea has an extensive air network, with seven domestic and eight international airports. Seoul is the primary air hub, served by two international airports – Gimpo and the newer Incheon, which opened in March 2002. Built on reclaimed land, Incheon International Airport is one of the world's largest, and it has ambitions to become the air transport hub of northeast Asia, with more than 60 cities of over a million people within two hours' flight time.

Asiana Airlines (one of Korea's two main carriers) prepares a plane at Incheon International Airport for a long-haul flight to London and New York. Incheon is a state-of-the-art airport built on reclaimed land and is set to become a major transport hub in eastern Asia.

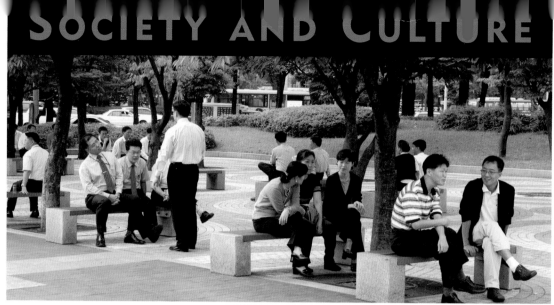

Office workers socialize during a lunch break in central Seoul.

The pace of change in South Korea's economy and population has had a profound impact on the daily lives of Koreans over the last three decades. Housing, health, education, leisure, and cultural values have all changed dramatically. Yet amid this change, South Korea's past is still very evident, and traditional values such as close-knit families remain strong.

FAMILY VALUES

The family has traditionally been the foundation of Korean communities. Families lived in the same house or nearby, under the guidance of the eldest male, who was respected and obeyed by all below him. Upon his death, the role of family leader would pass to his eldest son and so on down through the male side of the family. Females were historically less valued because they left their birth families upon marriage to become part of their husbands' families. Rapid industrialization and urbanization in South Korea have weakened the geographical proximity (closeness) of families, as different members have become dispersed across the country in search of job and housing opportunities. The social role of the

A bride dresses in traditional *hanbok* for her wedding. Weddings are a big family occasion and the trend for traditional-style ceremonies is on the increase.

family remains strong, however, and the patterns of respect and obedience continue, even over distance. Families still get together regularly – especially for key annual festivals such as Chuseok (the harvest moon festival) and family events such as weddings and *tol* (the celebration of the first birthday, which was a significant milestone before modern medicine improved infant mortality rates).

SENSE OF COMMUNITY

South Koreans' sense of community extends well beyond the family. They are well known for being very friendly and sociable people. Even everyday tasks, such as traveling to school or work, or shopping, are done with company. Almost everywhere you look, people are in conversation, sometimes with people they have only just met. In many other societies, the pressures of modern urban life have tended to erode (weaken) such strong social bonds, but in South Korea there is little sign of this. South Koreans have also been adept at using modern technology, such as mobile phones and text messaging, as another form of socializing. This is especially true of young people.

The press in South Korea is free and very active. Most adults will look at a newspaper at some point in the day.

CASE STUDY
THE CHAEBOL

The family structure prevades society and even forms the foundation of South Korea's most successful businesses – the *chaebols*. A *chaebol* is a conglomerate of companies that form a giant parent company. In South Korea, the *chaebols* include Samsung, Daewoo, Hyundai and LG. Most of South Korea's *chaebols* have developed from family-run businesses, with the parent company headed by the father, and the various sons (and other relatives) running the subsidiary companies. The government invested heavily in the *chaebols* as a way to encourage economic growth, but by the late 1990s it became clear that the *chaebols* had too much power. They not only controlled the largest manufacturing businesses, but also owned banks, housing corporations, social services, insurance companies, and transportation and tourism facilities. The government is now reforming business practices to allow others to compete, but the *chaebols* and their families still dominate almost every aspect of the economy.

45

The Seoul National University Hospital is South Korea's main hospital and was founded in 1885. It employs more than 3,700 people and serves around 2.25 million patients per year.

HEALTH AND WELL-BEING

South Koreans today enjoy a standard of health care comparable with that of other leading industrial countries, such as Japan, the United States and the United Kingdom, but many of the improvements are comparatively recent. In 1960, for example, when other industrialized nations already had life expectancies of around 70 years, South Koreans could expect a lifespan of just 54 years. By 2002, life expectancy had increased to 78 for women and 71 for men. Other health indicators have shown similar progress. For instance, infant mortality (children dying before their first birthday) fell from 9 percent of live births in 1960 to 0.5 percent by 2002.

EDUCATION

Free and compulsory education up to the end of middle school (16 years of age) has ensured South Korea has a well-educated population, with almost universal literacy. Education is highly valued and considered by

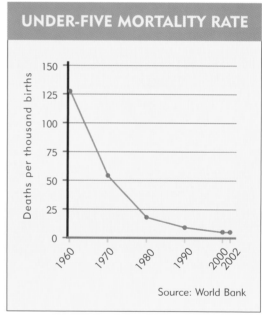

UNDER-FIVE MORTALITY RATE

Deaths per thousand births

Source: World Bank

most Koreans to be the best route to success. The government spends around 21 percent of its budget on education, compared with just 4 percent in the United Kingdom and only 2 percent in the United States. The school system is similar to that in other industrialized nations, with preschool (5–6 years of age), elementary school (7–12 years), middle school (13–16 years) and high school (16–19 years). Virtually all children complete

CASE STUDY
TRADITIONAL MEDICINE

Though modern medicine is widely available in South Korea, a considerable number of people continue to use traditional medicine known as *hanbang*, meaning "Korean prescription." *Hanbang* draws heavily on Chinese remedies and practices that were introduced in the sixth century. Acupuncture (*chi'im*), pressure point massage (*chiap*) and herbal remedies (*hanyak*) are among the different techniques used. *Hanyak* is particularly interesting and involves dozens of different natural ingredients, from roots, leaves, bark and fungi to nuts, fruits, honey, deer antlers, and dried centipedes! Each remedy is mixed from perhaps dozens of ingredients following a series of prescriptions contained in *Tong-ui pogam*, a 25-volume medical book first published in 1610. The ingredients are sold at traditional medicine pharmacies (*hanyakbang*) and at a select number of herbal markets. The largest of these markets are Yangyong Shijang in Daegu, which accounts for around 40 percent of all traditional medicine sales, and Gyeongdong in Seoul.

education through high school, and from there, around 70 percent will go on to higher education.

In addition to the formal education system, many children (and adults) take extra lessons, such as language courses. English is one of the most popular languages, as it is associated with better job opportunities. Language schools are found in almost all major towns, and there are even English language resorts where young Koreans can go to immerse themselves in an all-English-speaking environment.

OFFICIAL LANGUAGE

In 2004, Samsung announced that by 2008 it would adopt English as its official language, in the belief that this will improve its business opportunities.

All children study at elementary school (shown here) and middle school, and most continue through college or university.

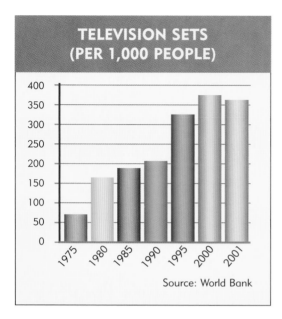

TELEVISION SETS (PER 1,000 PEOPLE)

Source: World Bank

TELECOMMUNICATIONS DATA (PER 1,000 PEOPLE)

Mainline phones	489
Mobile phones	679
Internet users	552

Source: World Bank

Ten-pin bowling is a popular pastime in South Korea.

LEISURE TIME

A shorter working week and higher disposable incomes have led to a boom in leisure and domestic tourism in South Korea. Improved health and the aging of the population have also contributed to these industries, as an increasing number of Koreans enjoy a more active retirement. Among the older generations, South Korea's numerous historic palaces and its beautiful national parks are particularly popular. City workers also seek these quiet refuges, and on fine weekends, the paths in more popular parks can seem almost as crowded as downtown Seoul.

Eating out, meeting in coffee bars, browsing around the shops, and going to the movies are all popular activities among young South Koreans. Movies have become so popular that an annual film festival was founded to celebrate Korean movies and the best of the foreign-made films. The Busan International Film Festival attracts huge audiences and many international stars. There is even a walk of fame, where film stars have left their handprints. In such a high-tech society, computer games, amusement arcades and the Internet are replacing many other forms of entertainment. In 2004, South Korea had the world's highest distribution of broadband Internet networks. The popularity of computer-based entertainment has led to concern about rising rates of computer addiction among younger people.

SPORTS

South Koreans enjoy keeping fit, and it is common to see people jogging, skating or cycling in city parks or exercising in public gymnasiums. The most popular sports in the country are soccer and baseball. Soccer received a huge boost when South Korea cohosted the 2002 World Cup finals with Japan. The unexpected success of the South Korean team – which made it to the semifinals – drove the country soccer crazy. South Korean athletes also excel in badminton, and their archers are the best in the world, carrying on a tradition in archery that dates back thousands of years. The traditional form of archery, called *goongdo,* is still practiced, along with other traditional Korean sports such as *ssireum* (wrestling) and *tae kwon do* (a martial art).

Enthusiasts practise traditional archery, called *goongdo,* at one of the only remaining ranges in Seoul. It is now protected as a culturally important site.

PERSONAL COMPUTERS (PER 1,000 PEOPLE)

Source: World Bank

CASE STUDY
CYWORLD

In 2004, there were an estimated 23.8 million 10–39 year olds using the Internet in South Korea. The main uses of the Internet are online gaming and cyber chat, and a number of companies have become specialists in meeting the huge demand. Cyworld is the most successful of these, with more than 10 million members since it was set up in September 2001. Cyworld offers users their own mini homepage, known as a "hompy," where they can place pictures, music, games, and web content, and a chat room to meet real or "virtual" friends. Each hompy also includes a "mini-room," which users can decorate with items bought from an online shop that also sells music and games. A new currency – acorns – has been created to purchase items in Cyworld, with one acorn being equivalent to 100 won (9 US cents). In October 2004, Cyworld was earning 150 million won a day from acorn sales alone.

49

TRADITIONAL CULTURE

In recent years, Korean culture and its unique traditions have enjoyed a resurgence. Traditional weddings are on the increase and so is interest in traditional sports. In fact, nearly all aspects of Korean culture are being reexamined by members of the present generation and carefully preserved for those of the future. Tourism has been an enormous boost to such efforts, generating interest in Korean practices from paper-making and traditional dance to costumes and food.

AN ACQUIRED TASTE

Korea's unique cuisine is based upon the historical availability of food supplies, and although many Western foods are now widely available (especially fast foods), local dishes are still dominant. Korea is surrounded by water, and fish and shellfish are a major part of the diet – normally eaten as soups, side dishes or dried snacks, rather than as a meal in itself. Meat has become part of the Korean diet in more recent times, with beef, chicken and pork all widely eaten. *Bulgogi* (thin strips of marinated beef) and *bulgalbi* (marinated beef ribs) are particularly popular, and Western fast-food companies have even created *bulgogi* burgers to appeal to Korean taste.

The two staples of the Korean diet are rice and *kimchi* (or *gimchi*). *Kimchi* is a seasoned and fermented vegetable – normally cabbage, turnip, radish or cucumber – that is eaten as an accompaniment with virtually every meal. There are around 200 varieties of *kimchi*, using different ingredients in the seasoning process such as garlic, chilies, salt, clams and anchovies. Winter *kimchi* was traditionally made in clay storage jars. These were partially buried to keep the fermenting ingredients at just the correct temperature. This process preserves the vegetables, allowing them to be eaten throughout the winter months, and *kimchi* jars are still in use today.

Kimchi (pickled and fermented vegetables) is considered the national dish of Korea and is available in hundreds of forms.

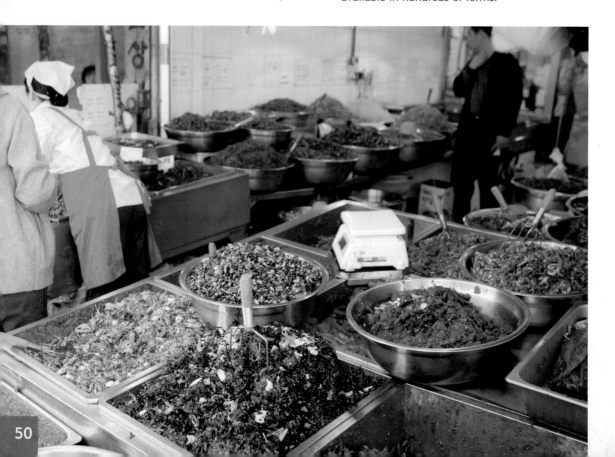

THE PAST ON SHOW

Many aspects of Korean culture are today largely for show. It is rare, for example, to see traditional dress (called *hanbok*) unless it is worn as part of a cultural performance or ceremony. Traditional dance and music, such as *nong-ak* (farmer's dance and music), is nowadays mainly performed at cultural shows for tourists. Most of South Korea's traditions are exhibited in cultural villages, such as the Korean Folk Village near Suwon, but in one or two places whole villages have been declared "folklore preservation zones." Here, people continue their lives as part of a living exhibit. One such village is Seongeup on Jeju-do, where traditional stone guardians (*harubang*) still protect a cluster of around 300 traditional buildings from evil spirits. Besides the traditional construction materials of stone walls and thatch-roped roofs, local customs are still used. Each house, for instance, has a stone post at either side of the entranceway, with three holes in each to hold poles that span the entrance. If all three poles are in place it means no one is home, so please stay away. If the top pole has one end lowered to the ground, the owners will be back soon. If all three poles have an end lowered it means they are at home and you are welcome.

ABOVE: The traditional farmer's dance is one of the most popular shows at the Korean Folk Village near Suwon.

BELOW: The gate poles of this traditional Korean homestead signal that the owner is home.

Rush-hour traffic in Seoul. As in other large cities, air pollution in Seoul is a major problem for the health of people living there.

The pressures of economic expansion and a growing population have taken their toll on South Korea's environment. There are problems of water and air pollution, habitat destruction and overuse of water resources. But South Koreans also show a strong appreciation of natural environments and flock by the thousand to the country's wilderness areas and national parks.

POLLUTION

South Korea's intensive use of resources for rapid economic growth creates various forms of pollution. In terms of air pollution, South Korea emitted more carbon dioxide (one of the major greenhouse gases) into the atmosphere than all but seven other countries. In context, however, this was still only 8 percent of the amount emitted by the United States, and in per-capita terms (the amount for each person) emissions are below the average for the OECD nations. But vehicle use and energy demands are rising. South Korea is taking measures to meet its future energy needs while minimizing any increase in carbon emissions. The investment in nuclear energy, for example, will eliminate the carbon dioxide

now produced by burning coal or natural gas. Vehicles are also being converted to run on propane, which produces far lower emissions than gasoline or diesel. A government program is set to replace 20,000 diesel buses with natural gas buses by 2007.

Water pollution is a growing concern. Agricultural chemicals are a major source of water pollution, and South Korea has one of the highest rates of fertilizer and pesticide use in the world: In 2003, an estimated 36.9 tonnes of nitrogen fertilizer and 1.43 tonnes of pesticide were applied per square kilometer of agricultural land. The United States, by comparison, applied less than 12 tonnes and 0.25 tonnes respectively. During the 1990s, the government began to acknowledge that water pollution had become a major problem. Chemicals from agricultural and industrial waste (including dangerous heavy metals such as cadmium and mercury) were contaminating water used for drinking and for watering crops. In 1998, the government introduced new water management measures, and by 2004, the water quality of South Korea's main rivers had stopped declining. The government is planning a water conservation project to take place between 2006 and 2015. This will place more limits on the acceptable levels of pollutants entering the water system.

Cardboard is collected from stores and restaurants in Seoul and taken to be sold for recycling.

CASE STUDY
SUSTAINABLE CITY

In 1978, the Nanjido district of Seoul was chosen as the landfill site for the waste generated by the rapidly growing city. An area of wildlife, lakes and wildflowers (Nanjido means "flower island"), it became a massive mountain of waste, with 93.5 million tonnes of industrial and municipal waste dumped there by 1993. This mass of waste created two massive plateaus more than 90 meters high and turned local streams into stinking, polluted wastelands. In 1994, a dramatic turnaround began at Nanjido. The plateaus of waste were stabilized and covered to form parkland and wilderness areas. The city also tapped energy from the site – using methane gas produced by the decomposing waste. Sustainable technologies – such as wind turbines and solar power – are being pioneered on the site, and recreation and education facilities encourage visitors to live a more sustainable lifestyle. An environmentally friendly residential area will complete Nanjido's transformation from garbage dump into a model of sustainable living.

Haneul Park in Nanjido is today a haven for wildlife and city dwellers, but until recently it was Seoul's biggest landfill site.

CASE STUDY
SAEMANGEUM WETLANDS

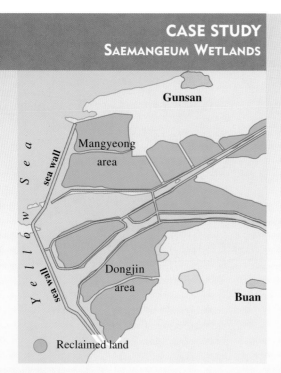

South Korea's most controversial environmental issue is the reclamation of the Saemangeum wetlands between Gunsan and Buan in the west. The wetlands are an important habitat for bird and fish species, including around 20,000 migratory birds that rest here on their journey between Australia and East Asia. Some of the bird species at Saemangeum are endangered, such as the spotted greenshank, of which there are fewer than 1,000 left in the world.

South Korea approved the plan to reclaim Saemangeum in the mid-1980s, with the intention that the new land would be used for agriculture to help meet growing food demands. Construction of the massive 33km seawall, designed to enclose the wetlands, began in 1991. By 2005, it was nearing completion, with less than 3km to finish. Environmental groups are concerned that the wall will disrupt the natural ecosystem and that draining the wetlands will destroy habitats and ruin the livelihoods of local shellfish farmers. Protests by environmental groups have periodically halted construction work at Saemangeum and forced the government to review the whole project. The government insists, however, that the project is environmentally friendly and will create new habitats for wildlife and recreation. It also argues that the additional farmland is essential to South Korea's future, as more and more land is engulfed by urban development. The outcome of Saemangeum (the world's largest ever reclamation project) – if and when it is completed – will be closely monitored and may well determine the future of other planned land reclamations in South Korea.

The Saemangeum wetlands, which at low tide stretch for miles, with the rising seawall visible in the distance. When the seawall is completed, this wetland will become fertile farmland.

PROTECTED AREAS

As early as 1967, South Korea recognized the need to protect its most fragile environments. Between then and 1988, the government established 20 national parks. Altogether, these cover around 6.6 percent of national territory, with a further 1.2 percent protected in the form of 22 provincial parks and 31 country parks. The Korea National Parks Authority was established in 1987 to manage the parks and introduce conservation programs. These programs include the careful monitoring of visitor impact and, if necessary, the temporary closure of some paths and park areas. With over 25 million visitors in 2003, the national parks have a unique opportunity to help encourage more sustainable ways of living. In 1999, the parks authority introduced an environmental education program using the assets of the national parks to educate visitors (and especially children) about the value of nature and methods of conserving it. The program holds nature experience classes, organizes nature-monitoring contests, and works with environmental groups to tackle specific issues of concern.

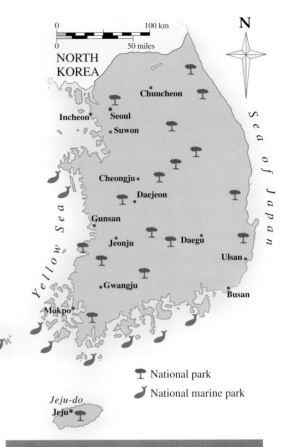

T National park

J National marine park

NATIONAL PARKS

SPECIES RICH

Although the national parks cover less than 7 percent of South Korea's area, 70 percent of the nation's 50,000–60,000 plant and animal species live within them. These include several endangered species such as the moon bear, otter, Korean red-headed woodpecker, brown serpent and longicorn beetle.

Tourists stream through the entrance to Seoraksan National Park at the peak of autumn colors in October – one of the busiest times of the year.

Economic success has brought a world of coffee bars, fashion and technology to young Koreans, but the economy must now keep up with fast-emerging China.

At the start of the twenty-first century, South Korea is entering a stage of maturity that will present its people with fresh challenges. The financial crisis of 1997 signaled the end of the country's honeymoon period and provided a shock to economy and people alike. The signs are that the Korean people are using their characteristic resolve and determination to overcome these challenges, but they know that others lie ahead.

FRESH COMPETITION

South Korea has firmly identified itself as one of the world's biggest economies and a major source of specialized engineering, consumer and electrical goods. It has overtaken countries such as Germany, the United States and Japan and come to dominate key sectors. However, it now faces perhaps its biggest challenge yet from China, one of its nearest neighbors. China is fast emerging as a major economic power and enjoying annual growth similar to that of South Korea in its boom years. The Chinese government is investing billions of dollars into its industries and utilizing the country's vast natural resources and cheap labor to undercut many of its competitors. China has already announced its intention to replace South Korea as the world's number-one shipbuilder by 2015 and is fast closing in on the lucrative electronics market, too. The government and businesses of South Korea recognize the threat posed by China and are seeking closer cooperation with China through initiatives such as the Yellow Sea Economic Basin (see page 37). It is hoped that such regional cooperation will help both nations to prosper.

SOCIAL CHANGE

The aging of the population will present South Korea with difficult choices in the coming years. The country will need to consider how to care for the older generations and also how to fill the void left in the younger working-age population. Economic immigration (especially from China) is one likely solution, but this could have profound and unforeseen effects on Korean culture. The government has been clamping down on illegal immigration, as it is aware that migrants may threaten the supply of South Korean jobs and raise unemployment.

UNIFICATION

The biggest challenge to the future of South Korea is the question of reunification with North Korea to form a single Korean nation.

The idea of a unified Korea seems almost universally popular in South Korea, but major obstacles and five decades of mistrust stand in the way. Talks between the two Koreas have stalled numerous times because of suspicions that North Korea is developing nuclear weapons. These suspicions were confirmed in 2003 when North Korea acknowledged it was developing a "nuclear deterrent." South Koreans' greatest fear is that the tension over North Korea's nuclear status could lead to another conflict on the peninsula, a conflict that could threaten millions of lives and damage South Korea's incredible achievements of the last 50 years.

South Korea's military remains on high alert in readiness against any threat from North Korea.

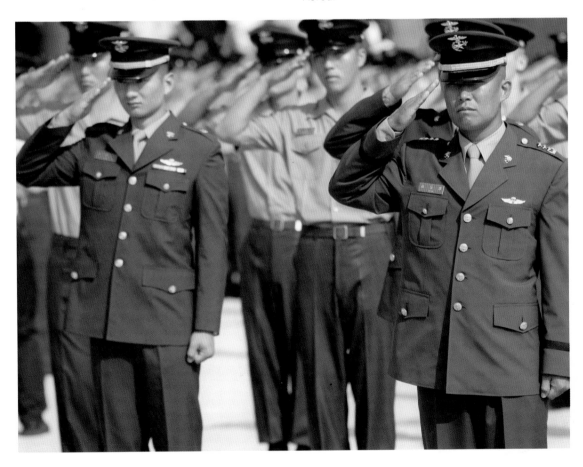

Aquaculture The farming of aquatic goods (such as fish, seaweed, or shellfish) in artificial ponds or large enclosures submerged in the sea or a lake.

Biotechnology The manipulation of natural species for human gain. Methods include cross-breeding of plants and animals (hybridization) and, more recently, modifying genes using genetic engineering.

Chaebol The Korean term for a large business empire that is connected to a single family.

Cinder cone A cone of debris that forms around the vent of a volcano during an eruption.

Cold War An ideological struggle between communism (led by the Soviet Union) and capitalist free-market democracy (led by the United States) that took place 1945–91.

Consumer electronics Electrical products used by the general public, such as computers, cameras, televisions, and DVD and CD players.

Cottage industry A small-scale industry employing just a few people at a local level and often related to traditional crafts, such as pottery, paper-making or weaving.

Demilitarized Zone (DMZ) An area between South and North Korea established along the cease-fire line between the two countries in 1953. It is 248km long and 4km wide and acts as a buffer between the two opposing military forces.

Ecosystem The contents of an environment, including all the plants and animals that live there. This can be tiny or as large as planet Earth.

Floodplain Wide, flat areas surrounding a river, typically in the lower reaches, that naturally flood in periods of high river flow. The floods deposit rich sediments, producing fertile soils.

GDP (gross domestic product) The monetary value of goods and services produced by a country in a single year, often measured per person (capita) as GDP per capita.

Geological uplift The process by which land is forced upward by processes in the Earth's crust, such as volcanic activity and the collision of the Earth's tectonic plates.

GNI (gross national income) The monetary value of the goods and services produced by a country plus any earnings from overseas in a single year, often measured per person (capita) as GNI per capita.

Heavy industry Large and often key industries, such as steelworks, shipbuilding, and construction and engineering.

Homogeneous Being uniform or very similar in nature. In South Korea, this term is often applied to its population.

Hydroelectric power (HEP) Electricity generated by water as it passes through turbines. These normally involve large dams across river valleys that form artificial lakes behind them.

Immigrant A person who has moved into a new area, especially into a new country.

Industrialization The process by which a country moves away from an economy based upon agriculture or resource extraction and becomes more industrial in nature.

Infrastructure The lines of transportation and communication necessary for an economy and society to function efficiently. These include roads, railroads, electricity lines, water pipes, sewers, telephone lines, ports, airports and so on.

International Monetary Fund (IMF) An organization that assists governments during periods of economic uncertainty or shock by providing loans. The IMF is designed to encourage a stable world economy.

Land reclamation The process of converting an area (often a wetland or shallow coastal region) into usable land for agriculture, housing or other economic activity. This is normally done by drainage or infilling.

Lava tube A pipelike structure or cave made of hardened lava, through which molten lava once flowed.

Migrant Someone who has moved into or out of an area.

Nanotechnology Technology developed at a very small scale to perform specialized functions.

Newly industrialized country (NIC) A term used to describe a number of countries with rapidly industrializing economies that emerged during the 1970s in Asia and South America.

Silver towns Settlements where retired South Koreans are moving to enjoy their later years. They have the necessary practical and leisure facilities, such as stores, health clinics and golf courses.

Subtropical Describes a climate that is tropical for part of the year or almost tropical for the whole year. Subtropical regions often support vegetation more normally found in tropical regions.

Sustainable technology Technology that brings benefits to people today without damaging the environment for future generations.

Temperate Describes the dominant climatic conditions found between the latitudes of the Tropics and the polar circles. Within this zone, great variations in temperature can be experienced.

Tidal range The difference in height between the high and low tide marks. In South Korea, the west coast has a very large tidal range, but on the east coast it is very slight.

Typhoon A violent tropical storm in the western Pacific Ocean, known as a hurricane in other parts of the world.

FURTHER INFORMATION

BOOKS TO READ:

Nilsen, Robert. *Moon Handbooks: South Korea.* 3d ed. Emeryville, Ca.: Moon Publications, 2004. A travel guidebook with extensive historical notes on the provinces and noteworthy locations of South Korea.

Salter, Christopher L. *Modern World Nations: South Korea.* Updated ed. Philadelphia: Chelsea House, 2005. An illustrated study of the land, people, and history of South Korea and its position in the world today.

Winchester, Simon. *Korea: A Walk Through the Land of Miracles.* New York: Perennial, 2005. An engaging account by the well-known historian of his walk across South Korea, from the southern shore to the Demilitarized Zone.

WEBSITES:

CIA World Factbook
http://cia.gov/cia/publications/factbook/geos/ks.html
The US Central Intelligence Agency's online factbook, with statistics and assessments of all countries of the world.

Korea National Parks Authority
http://www.npa.or.kr/eng/main.htm
Information and statistics in English about the parks service.

Korea National Statistical Office
http://www.nso.go.kr/eng/
Useful statistical information about all aspects of Korea. Presented in English and clearly organized.

Korea.net: Gateway to Korea
http://www.kois.go.kr/
General information on life in South Korea as well as news on government, tourism, business, and sports.

Seoul Metropolitan Government
http://english.seoul.go.kr
Plenty of informative content about the South Korean capital.

Television Trust for the Environment
http://www.tve.org/news/doc.cfm?aid=1190
Information about the Saemangeum wetlands and the project to reclaim them for agricultural and industrial use.

METRIC CONVERSION TABLE

To convert	to	do this
mm (millimeters)	inches	divide by 25.4
cm (centimeters)	inches	divide by 2.54
m (meters)	feet	multiply by 3.281
m (meters)	yards	multiply by 1.094
km (kilometers)	yards	multiply by 1094
km (kilometers)	miles	divide by 1.6093
kilometers per hour	miles per hour	divide by 1.6093
cm^2 (square centimeters)	square inches	divide by 6.452
m^2 (square meters)	square feet	multiply by 10.76
m^2 (square meters)	square yards	multiply by 1.196
km^2 (square kilometers)	square miles	divide by 2.59
km^2 (square kilometers)	acres	multiply by 247.1
hectares	acres	multiply by 2.471
cm^3 (cubic centimeters)	cubic inches	multiply by 16.387
m^3 (cubic meters)	cubic yards	multiply by 1.308
l (liters)	pints	multiply by 2.113
l (liters)	gallons	divide by 3.785
g (grams)	ounces	divide by 28.329
kg (kilograms)	pounds	multiply by 2.205
metric tonnes	short tons	multiply by 1.1023
metric tonnes	long tons	multiply by 0.9842
BTUs (British thermal units)	kWh (kilowatt-hours)	divide by 3,415.3
watts	horsepower	multiply by 0.001341
kWh (kilowatt-hours)	horsepower-hours	multiply by 1.341
MW (megawatts)	horsepower	multiply by 1,341
gigawatts per hour	horsepower per hour	multiply by 1,341,000
°C (degrees Celsius)	°F (degrees Fahrenheit)	multiply by 1.8 then add 32

Detail from a drum used during the changing of the guard at Changdeokgung (Palace of Illustrious Virtue), Seoul.

A giant Buddha dominates the
Shinheung-sa temple complex
within Seoraksan National Park
in the northeast of the country.